Daisy's Dancing Lesson

Gill Munton

Series Editor: Louis Fidge

Contents

Daisy's dancing lesson

Daisy said, 'I like your pink dress, Suzy.'

Suzy said, 'I go to dancing lessons.
This is the dress I wear.'

At bedtime, Daisy said,
'Suzy goes to dancing lessons.
Can I go to dancing lessons, too?'

Mum said, 'Yes, you can.'

Daisy went to a dancing lesson.

The teacher said, 'I want you all to be birds. Wave your arms, like birds.'

The teacher played the piano.
All the little dinosaurs waved their
arms like birds.

The teacher said, 'You are a very good
bird, Suzy. You are very good, too, Harry.'

The teacher said, 'Now I want you all
to be horses. Run round the room, like horses.'

The teacher played the piano. All the little dinosaurs ran round the room like horses.

The teacher said, 'You are a very good horse, Suzy. You are very good, too, Freddy.'

Daisy said, 'I can't do it!'

The teacher said, 'Now I want you all
to be frogs. Jump up and down, like frogs.'

The teacher played the piano.
All the little dinosaurs jumped up
and down like frogs.

The teacher said, 'Daisy. You are not
a good frog. Try harder.'

Daisy said, 'I can't do it! I want to
go home. I don't like dancing lessons.'

The teacher said, 'Now I want you all
to stand on one leg like storks.'

All the little dinosaurs stood like storks.

The teacher said, 'Now I want you all to spin round and round, like wheels.'

She played the piano.
All the little dinosaurs started to spin.

Wheeeee!

Daisy spun across the room.
She spun out of the door.

She said, 'Help! I can't stop!'

Daisy said, 'Look, Mum. I can spin.
I can spin round and round.'

The teacher and all the little dinosaurs
came to look.

The teacher said, 'Look at Daisy.
Give Daisy a big clap.'

'Did you like your dancing lesson?'
Mum said.

Daisy said, 'Yes. I can't be a bird,
and I can't be a horse,
and I can't be a frog.
But I can stand on one leg like a stork
and spin round and round like a wheel.
When is my next dancing lesson?'

I can fly like a bird,
I can fly, fly, fly.
I can fly like a bird
in the sky, sky, sky.

I can run like a horse,
I can run, run, run.
I can run like a horse
in the sun, sun, sun.

I can jump like a frog,
I can jump and hop.
I can jump like a frog
to the top, top, top.

I can stand like a stork,
One foot on the ground.
I can spin like a wheel
and go round and round.

What can **you** do?
Can you fly?
Can you run?
Can you hop?
Can you spin?

Daisy and the dentist

Mum said, 'It's time to go to the dentist!'

Daisy said, 'I don't want to go.
I don't like the dentist.'

Mum said, 'It's good to go to the dentist.
He looks after your teeth.'

Then Daisy said,
'I can't go to the dentist.
Look at my bedroom.
I must clean it.'

Mum said, 'Come on, Daisy.
We're going to the dentist,
and we're going now.
Get your coat.'

Daisy got her coat.

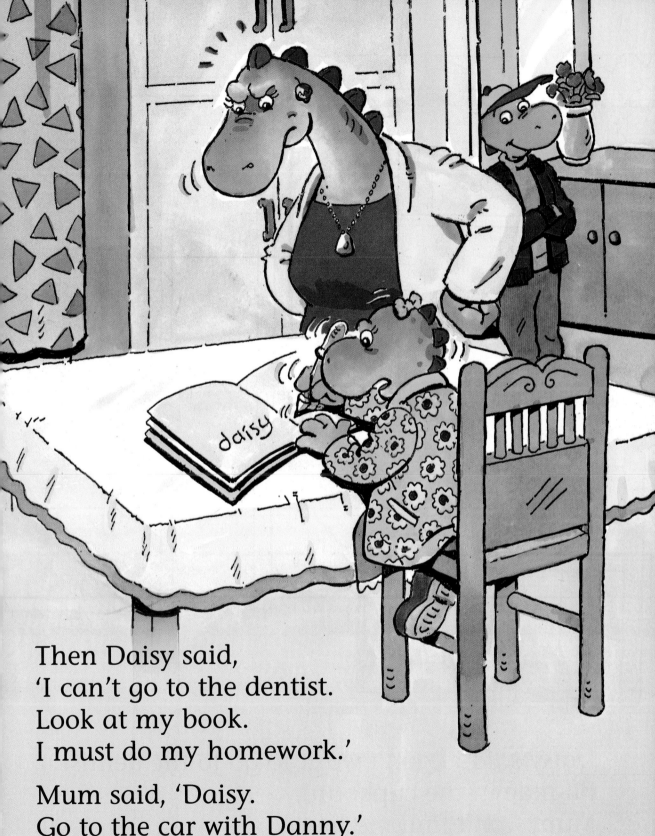

Then Daisy said,
'I can't go to the dentist.
Look at my book.
I must do my homework.'

Mum said, 'Daisy.
Go to the car with Danny.'

Daisy said, 'I don't want to go to the dentist.
I'll hide in the cupboard.
Mum won't find me here.'

Danny went to the car.

Mum looked for her keys.

Mum went to the cupboard to get her keys.
She saw Daisy.

Mum said, 'Daisy! Why are you hiding?'

Daisy said, 'I'm hiding because I don't want
to go to the dentist.'

Mum said, 'Don't be scared, Daisy.
The dentist is a very nice man.'

A nurse opened the door.

The nurse said, 'Come in, Daisy.
Come in, Danny.'

Daisy said, 'I don't want to come in.
I want to go home.'

The nurse said, 'This is Daisy.'

The dentist said, 'Hello, Daisy.
Come and sit in my chair.'

Daisy sat in the chair.
The chair went up and down.

Daisy said, 'I like your chair.'

The dentist said, 'Open your mouth, Daisy.
I want to look at your teeth.'

Daisy opened her mouth.

The dentist looked at Daisy's teeth.

'Very good,' he said.

Then he cleaned them with pink toothpaste.

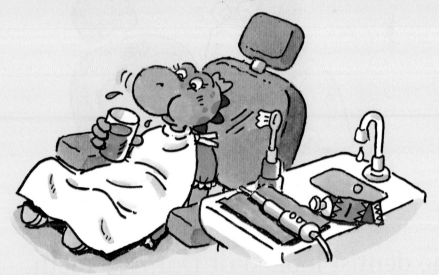

The dentist said, 'Now wash your mouth.'

Daisy washed her mouth.

The dentist said, 'You can go now, Daisy.
It's time to look at Danny's teeth.'

The dentist looked at Danny's teeth.

He said, 'Oh, dear!
Too many sweets, Danny!'

Soon it was time to go home.

Daisy said, 'I like the dentist.
I like his chair, and the pink toothpaste.
When can I go to the dentist again?'

At the dentist

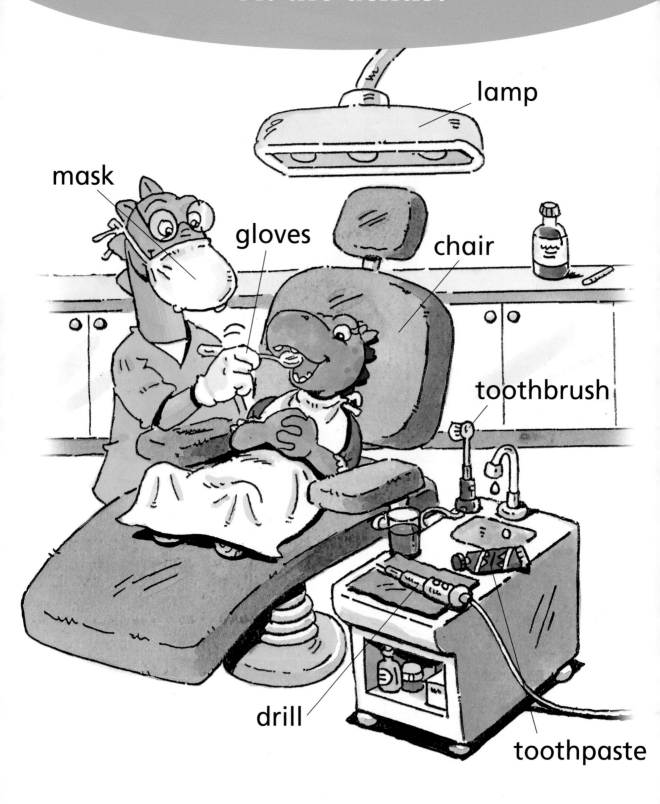

lamp

mask

gloves

chair

toothbrush

drill

toothpaste

These are good for your teeth.
Eat lots of them.

These are bad for your teeth.
Don't eat too many of them.

Word list

a	dear	homework	oh	the
across	dentist	horse(s)	on	their
after	did	I	one	them
again	dinosaurs	I'll	open/opened	then
all	do/don't	I'm	out	this
and	door	in	piano	time
are	down	is	pink	to
arms	dress	it	played	too
around	find	it's	ran	toothpaste
at	for	jump/jumped	room	try
be	Freddy	keys	round	up
because	frog(s)	leg	run	very
bedroom	get	lesson(s)	said	want
bedtime	give	like	sat	was
big	go	little	saw	wash
bird(s)	goes	look/looked	scared	washed
book	going	looks	she	wave/waved
but	good	man	sit	we're
came	got	many	soon	wear
can/can't	harder	me	spin	went
car	Harry	mouth	spun	wheel(s)
chair	he	Mum	stand	when
clap	hello	must	started	why
clean/cleaned	help	my	stood	with
coat	her	next	stop	won't
come	here	nice	stork(s)	yes
cupboard	hide	not	Suzy	you
Daisy	hiding	now	sweets	your
dancing	his	nurse	teacher	
Danny	home	of	teeth	

Language structures

Imperatives:
Wave your arms.
Don't be scared.

Preposition *like*:
Wave your arms, like birds.

***want to*:**
I want to go home.
I don't want to come in.

Prepositions of movement:
across, out of, round,
up and down

***must*:**
I must do my homework.

***will/won't*:**
I'll hide in the cupboard.
Mum won't find me here.

***why/because*:**
Why are you hiding?
… because I don't want to go
to the dentist.

***can/can't*:**
I can stand on one leg
I can't be a horse.

Requests with *can*:
Can I go to dancing lessons?

Adverb *too*:
You are very good, too …

Adjectives:
scared, nice, good

***too many*:**
too many sweets

Comparisons:
Try harder.